Bond

English
10 Minute Tests

8–9 years

Sarah Lindsay

OXFORD
UNIVERSITY PRESS

TEST 1: Mixed

Test time: 0 — 5 — 10 minutes

Add the *suffix* able or ible to each of these to make a word.

1 excit*able*
2 flex*ible*
3 agree*able*
4 forgiv*able*
5 revers*ible*
6 avoid*able*

Change the underlined words into a *pronoun*.

7 The new puppy is <u>my puppy</u>.
   The new puppy is *mine*.

8 The red sports car is <u>the Frost family's</u>.
   The red sports car is *theirs*.

9 Her house is next to <u>our house</u>.
   Her house is next to *ours*.

10 The coat on the ground is <u>Jacob's</u>.
   The coat on the ground is *is his*.

2

Write an *antonym* for each word.

11 scream   whisper

12 stand   move

13 build   break

14 smile   frown

15 quiet   noise

16 outside inside

Copy these sentences and add the missing punctuation.

17 "Have you fed the dog this morning?" asked Mum.

18 Dad moaned, "Time I mowed the lawn again."

19 "Can we go swimming this afternoon?" Alex and Tom pleaded.

20 Poppy said, "I can't wait until your birthday party."

Test 2: Spelling

Test time: 0 – 5 – 10 minutes

Add gue or que to complete these words.

1. lea _gue_
2. uni _que_
3. anti _que_
4. ton _gue_

Circle the silent letter in each of these words.

5. fas(c)inate
6. cres(c)ent
7. s(c)ent
8. dis(c)ipline
9. s(c)issors
10. s(c)ience

Add the missing double letters to each of these words.

11. fla _n n_ el
12. spa _r r_ ow
13. ye _l l_ ow
14. ke _t t_ le
15. sa _d d_ le
16. wri _g g_ le
17. po _l l_ ute
18. le _s s_ on

Spell each of these words correctly. Some need a letter added, some need a letter changed.

19. sc*h*eme
20. ma*c*hine
21. *ch*aracter
22. bro*c*hure
23. shel*f*
24. ec*h*o
25. c*h*orus

4

Total

TEST 3: Spelling

Write a *homophone* for each of these words.

1. knew — new
2. seen — scene
3. bored — board
4. sighed — side
5. source — sauce
6. dear — deer
7. piece — peace

Write each of these *nouns* in their *plural* form.

8. church — churches
9. valley — vallys
10. knife — knives
11. baby — babies
12. clock — clocks
13. café — cafes
14. kilo — kilos
15. dish — dishes

Circle the correct spelling of each word.

16. (height) hieght
17. aweful (awful)
18. (favourite) favorite
19. quater (quarter)
20. naghty (naughty)
21. adress (address)
22. (famous) famos
23. (various) varius
24. (library) libary
25. roze (rose)

TEST 4: **Comprehension**

> Read this extract carefully.

The Best Birthday Present
by Ruud van der Rol and Rian Verhoeven

1 Anne Frank woke early at six o'clock in the morning on Friday, 12th June. She could hardly wait to get out of bed. That she was up so early was not surprising, since today
5 was her thirteenth birthday.

It was wartime, 1942. Anne was living with her father and mother and her sister, Margot, who was three years older than Anne, in a housing development
10 in Amsterdam, the capital city of the Netherlands. The Netherlands had been occupied for two years by the Germans, who had launched a campaign of discrimination and persecution against the
15 Jews. It was becoming increasingly difficult for Jews such as the Frank family to lead ordinary lives, but Anne was not thinking about that on her birthday.

At seven o'clock she went to her parents'
20 bedroom. Then the whole family gathered together in the living room to unwrap Anne's presents.

Anne received many gifts that day, including books, a jigsaw puzzle, a
25 brooch, and candy. But her best present was one given by her parents that morning: a hardcover diary, bound in red and white checkered cloth. She had never had a diary before and was delighted
30 with the gift. Anne had many friends, both boys and girls, but with them she talked only about everyday things. But now Anne's diary would be her very best friend, a friend she could trust with
35 everything. She called her new friend "Kitty".

I hope I shall be able to confide in you completely, as I have never been able to do in anyone before, and I hope that you will be a
40 *great support and comfort to me.* Anne Frank (12 June 1942)

On the inside of the cover she stuck a photograph of herself, and wrote next to it: *Gorgeous photo, isn't it!!!*

45 Anne started writing to Kitty in her diary two days later, on Sunday, June 14. She would continue filling it for just over two years with her thoughts and feelings, and stories about all the things
50 that happened to her. But on that first day, she could not suspect how her life was suddenly to change completely. Nor could she imagine that later millions of people throughout the world would read
55 her diary.

Anne and her family went into hiding on 6 July 1942 in fear that if they didn't, the Germans would arrest and possibly kill them. They stayed in hiding for more than two years until they were finally betrayed. When the Franks were taken away by the Germans, Anne's diary was left behind. Only Anne's father survived the war and he had her diary published in 1947.

Answer these questions about the extract.

1. Why was 12th June an important day for Anne?

2. Where did Anne live?

3. How much older than Anne was her sister?

4. What was Anne's 'best present'?

5. Why do you think Anne was so delighted with this present?

6. For how long did Anne write to 'Kitty'?

7. What is meant by 'The Netherlands had been occupied for two years by the Germans' (lines 11–12)?

8. Anne's diary is now very famous and read by millions of people. How do you think Anne would have felt about this?

Test 5: **Vocabulary**

Test time: 0 — 5 — 10 minutes

Write these words in *alphabetical order*.

> garlic   garden   gangster   garage   gateau

1 (1) _gangster_

2 (2) _garage_

3 (3) _____

4 (4) _____

5 (5) _____

Write a *definition* for each of these words.

6 school

_____

7 tube

_____

8 rabbit

_____

9 adult

_____

10 hour

_____

Draw a line to match a word in the first column with a word in the second column to make a *compound word*.

11–15 any   head

　　　　　card   room

　　　　　red   where

　　　　　water   board

　　　　　class   fall

Write a *synonym* for each word.

16 active _____

17 angry   _____

18 run   _____

19 repair _____

20 hate   _____

Test 6: Mixed

Add the missing apostrophes to each sentence.

1. Let's have a race!
2. I'll remember to bring my book.
3. There's another way to get to the park.
4. What shall I say we've been doing?
5. I can't believe we are lost again!

Write these sentences in their *plural* form.

Example: The person walked into the shop. *The people walked into the shops.*

6. The dog chased the ball.
   _____

7. School is closed on Tuesday.
   _____

8. The Sun shone and made the flower grow.
   _____

9. The car sped down the country lane.
   _____

Circle the masculine words.

10–14　　prince　　　　duchess　　　　queen

　　　　　gander　　　　duke　　　　　　nephew

　　　　　madam　　　　waiter　　　　　niece

Add the missing 'y' to each of these words.

15　rhme　　　　_____

16　mstery　　　_____

17　gm　　　　 _____

18　phsical　　 _____

19　mth　　　　_____

20　encclopedia _____

TEST 7: **Grammar**

Test time: 0 — 5 — 10 minutes

Underline the *verb* in each line.

1	he	dog	flap	sadly	hive
2	kite	hill	scream	they	brown
3	when	growl	bucket	lovely	sister
4	scratch	biro	on	bungalow	you

Write an interesting *adjective* to describe each of these *nouns*.

5 a _____ gate

6 a _____ house

7 a _____ lamb

8 a _____ bike

9 a _____ T-shirt

Write two examples of an *adverb*.

10–11 _____   _____

Rewrite the *proper nouns* with capital letters.

mobile phone	chicken	roald dahl
jupiter	homework	biscuit
tower of london	computer	banana

12 _____

13 _____

14 _____

Write one of the following *conjunctions* in each gap so that every sentence makes sense. Each word may be used only once.

| because | and | after | so | but | while |

15 Hannah held Ben's bike _____ he went into the shop.

16 Veejay had his tea _____ finishing his homework.

17 Aimee enjoys going to Dancing Club _____ loves Gym Club more.

18 Dan ran home from school _____ he wanted to watch something on television.

19 A loudspeaker was used by Mrs Golding _____ all the children could hear clearly.

20 Mum made the sandwiches _____ then put them in the rucksack.

Test 8: Comprehension

Read this extract carefully.

The Butterfly Lion *by Michael Morpurgo*

1 *Bertie was born in South Africa, in a remote farmhouse near a place called Timbavati.*

One evening – Bertie must have been six years old by now – he was sitting high up in the branches of a tree, hoping against hope the lions might come down for their sunset drink as they often did. He was thinking of giving up, for it would soon be too dark to see much now, when he saw a solitary lioness come down to the waterhole. Then he saw that she was not alone. Behind her, and on unsteady legs, came what looked like a lion cub – but it was white, glowing white in the gathering gloom of dusk.

While the lioness drank, the cub played at catching her tail; and then, when she had had her fill, the two of them slipped away into the long grass and were gone.

Bertie ran inside, screaming with excitement. He had to tell someone, anyone. He found his father working at his desk.

"Impossible," said his father. "You're seeing things that aren't there, or you're telling fibs – one of the two."

"I saw him. I promise," Bertie insisted.

But his father would have none of it, and sent him to his room for arguing.

His mother came to see him later.

"Anyone can make a mistake, Bertie dear," she said. "It must have been the sunset. It plays tricks with your eyes sometimes. There's no such thing as a white lion."

The next evening Bertie watched again at the fence, but the white lion cub and the lioness did not come, nor did they the next evening, nor the next.

Bertie began to think he must have been dreaming it.

A week or more passed, and there had been only a few zebras and wildebeest down at the waterhole. Bertie was already upstairs in his bed when he heard his father riding into the compound, and then the stamp of his heavy boots on the veranda.

"We got her! We got her!" he was saying. "Huge lioness, massive she was. She's taken half a dozen of my best cattle in the last two weeks. Well, she won't be taking any more."

Bertie's heart stopped. In that one terrible moment he knew which lioness his father was talking about. There could be no doubt in it. His white lion cub had been orphaned.

Answer these questions about the extract.

1. In which country did Bertie live?
   _____

2. Where was Bertie sitting while waiting for the lions?
   _____

3. What was so special about the lion cub Bertie spotted that evening?
   _____

4. Why did Bertie's dad send Bertie to his room?
   _____
   _____
   _____

5. What other animals does Bertie see at the waterhole?
   _____

6. Why did Bertie begin to doubt what he'd seen?
   _____
   _____

7. Which line in the extract tells how Bertie felt on hearing the news the lioness had been killed?
   _____

8. What do you think Bertie does next?
   _____
   _____

Time for a break! Go to Puzzle Page 39

Test 9: Mixed

Rewrite this short passage, adding the missing capital letters.

1–6 najib called to his friend, "quick, if we don't hurry we will miss the party!" henry wasn't sure he wanted to go all the way to stafford but he grabbed his jumper anyway. "coming, i'm coming," he moaned.

_____

_____

_____

_____

_____

_____

Add its or it's to each gap in the sentences.

7   _____ a very sunny day.

8   Look at the baby bird on the ground. How will it find _____ nest?

9   The puppy has chewed my slippers again. _____ getting beyond a joke!

10 The school has _____ playground at the back of the building.

Circle the *collective nouns*.

11–13　mouse　　　gate　　　　Portsmouth

　　　　bouquet　　Hannah　　tribe

　　　　lantern　　　glass　　　box

　　　　flock　　　　poodle　　building

Add ory, ary or ery to make a word.

14　deliv_____

15　prim_____

16　machin_____

17　mem_____

18　Janu_____

19　laborat_____

20　discov_____

TEST 10: **Spelling**

Test time: 0 — 5 — 10 minutes

Add the *prefix* re, un, non or dis to each of these words.

1 _____sense

2 _____call

3 _____fair

4 _____aware

5 _____honest

6 _____continue

7 _____visit

8 _____ability

Put a tick next to the words spelt correctly and a cross next to those spelt incorrectly.

9   weigh   _____

10 thuoght _____

11 vien   _____

12 double   _____

13 tuch   _____

14 nieghbour _____

15 country _____

16 truble   _____

17 yuong   _____

18 they   _____

Add the *suffix* to each word. Don't forget any necessary spelling changes.

19 expand + sion   _____

20 simple + ly   _____

21 magic + ian   _____

22 angry + ly   _____

23 confuse + sion   _____

24 prepare + tion   _____

25 televise + sion   _____

18

Test 11: **Spelling**

Test time: 0 — 5 — 10 minutes

Add the *suffix* ous to these root words. Watch out, some of the root words need to change.

1. poison _____
2. outrage _____
3. mountain _____
4. joy _____
5. peril _____

6. vigor _____
7. danger _____
8. nerve _____
9. humour _____
10. courage _____

Add the *suffix* tion or sion to make a word.

11. frac_____
12. inva_____
13. direc_____
14. deci_____

15. men_____
16. occa_____
17. televi_____
18. subtrac_____

Add ie or ei to each of these to make a word.

19. th _ _ f
20. p _ _ ce
21. f _ _ ld
22. w _ _ gh

23. _ _ ght
24. v _ _ n
25. c _ _ ling

19

Total

TEST 12: **Sentences**

Test time: 0 — 5 — 10 minutes

Add the missing punctuation to the end of each sentence.

1 Why haven't I been given a present ___

2 The team waited in line to board the coach ___

3 Watch out, that car is heading for you ___

4 Do you want to borrow my bike ___

5 I think I'm stuck, help ___

6 Mum put the glass of water on the table ___

Copy these sentences, adding the missing speech marks.

7 Tania whispered, Quiet or we will wake Grandad.

   _____

   _____

8 Where is the best place to fish? Tom asked Yousef.

   _____

   _____

9 Helen giggled, Why are you wearing that strange-looking hat?

   _____

   _____

10 I love you, said Seamus as he cuddled his puppy.

   _____

   _____

Make a noun phrase for each of these nouns and add it to a sentence.

11 spider

_____

_____

12 baby

_____

_____

13 car

_____

_____

14 shadow

_____

_____

Add the missing apostrophes in these _phrases_.

15 the two horses reins

16 the four boys hats

17 the five pupils books

18 the Prime Ministers socks

19 the twelve cars wheels

20 the old mans shoes

Time for a break! Go to Puzzle Page 40

Leisure Centre, Pleasure Centre *by John Rice*

1   You go through plate glass doors
    with giant red handles,
    into light that's as bright
    as a million candles.
5   The chlorine smells
    the whole place is steaming,
    the kids are yelling
    and the kids are screaming.

    Watch them
10 wave jump
    dive thump
    cartwheel
    free wheel
    look cute
15 slip chute
    toe stub
    nose rub
    in the leisure centre, pleasure centre.

    Sporty people laugh and giggle
20 folk in swimsuits give a wiggle.
    Kids are in the café busy thinking
    if they can afford some fizzy drinking.
    In the changing rooms
    wet folk shiver.
25 It's hard to get dressed
    when you shake and quiver.

    And we go
    breast stroke
    back stroke
30 two stroke

    big folk
    hair soak
    little folk
    eye poke
35 no joke
    in the leisure centre, pleasure centre.

    And now we are driving back home
    fish 'n' chips in the car,
    eyes are slowly closing
40 but it's not very far.
    Snuggle wuggle up in fresh clean sheets
    a leisure centre trip
    is the best of treats because you can
    keep fit
45 leap sit
    eat crisps
    do twists
    belly flop
    pit stop
50 fill up
    with 7-Up
    get going
    blood flowing
    look snappy
55 be happy
    in the leisure centre, pleasure centre.

Answer these questions about the poem.

1 What is this poem about?

_____

2 List three things the poet notices as he goes into the leisure centre.

_____

_____

3 Find a word in the poem rhyming with 'chute'.

_____

4 What are the children in the café thinking?

_____

5 Why is it hard to get dressed?

_____

6 What does the line 'eyes are slowly closing' (line 39) describe?

_____

7 List three things mentioned in the poem that children might not enjoy while at the leisure centre.

_____

_____

8 Why is the poem titled 'Leisure Centre, Pleasure Centre'?

_____

_____

_____

TEST 14: **Mixed**

Test time: 0 — 5 — 10 minutes

Draw a line to match the words in each column that have the same letter string and pronunciation.

1   thorough   bough

2   rough   dough

3   nought   borough

4   though   thought

5   plough   tough

Write a *definition* for each of these words.

6   dictionary

_____

7   diary

_____

8   ordinary

_____

9   February

_____

10   boundary

_____

24

Underline the *conjunctions* in each sentence.

11 At last Dad arrived home <u>so</u> we could eat our tea.

12 The wind rustled in the trees <u>as</u> darkness fell.

13 Jemma concentrated hard on her game of chess <u>because</u> it was an important match.

14 Daxa picked up the bags <u>and</u> carried them into the house.

15 The phone rang <u>but</u> nobody was home.

Add the missing commas to these sentences.

16 Lia packed her hairbrush, nightie and toothbrush.

17 Despite the tent being hot and stuffy, Abi found it fairly comfortable.

18–19 When Daniel returned from school he did his homework, piano practice, walked the dog and cleaned the fish tank.

20 Sarah ran down the lane, her school bag bumping against her leg.

TEST 15: **Vocabulary**

Write an *antonym* for each word.

1 start _____
2 push _____
3 happy _____
4 reward _____
5 flexible _____

Write these words in *alphabetical order*.

tartan   tarantula   tarnish   target   tart

6 (1) _____
7 (2) _____
8 (3) _____
9 (4) _____
10 (5) _____

Write the *diminutive* for each of these animals.

11 duck _____
12 pig _____
13 goose _____

Write two sentences for this *homonym*. In each sentence the *homonym* must have a different meaning.

14–15 mine

(1) _____

_____

_____

(2) _____

_____

_____

The words used to describe something can change over time. Draw a line to match the words in each column that mean the same.

	Words used today	Words used in the past
16	dress	pitcher
17	glasses	satchel
18	schoolbag	wireless
19	radio	spectacles
20	jug	frock

27

TEST 16: **Mixed**

Test time: 0 — 5 — 10 minutes

Change each of these *plural* words into its *singular* form.

1 engines _____

2 foxes   _____

3 flies   _____

4 scarves _____

5 drums   _____

Add an *adjectival phrase* to complete each sentence.

6 The _____

   car stopped quickly as the children began to cross the road.

7 Jess's camping party was great fun but we all got very wet in the

   _____ rain.

8 The _____ lambs

   raced across the field.

9 Callum always enjoyed picking the _____

   _____ blackberries.

28

Add sure or ture to each of these to make a word.

10 expo_____

11 ma_____

12 signa_____

13 displea_____

14 minia_____

15 pres_____

Add the missing apostrophes.

16 Kates homework

17 my countrys flag

18 Liams computer

19 Meenas cakes

20 the birds nests

TEST 17: **Grammar**

Test time: 0 — 5 — 10 minutes

Underline the *adverbs* in these sentences.

1 The machinery clunked noisily before grinding to a stop.

2 The old lady walked awkwardly on the icy path.

3 Tess dressed sleepily after her alarm woke her.

4 Sanjay hastily ate his tea so he could join his friends outside.

Write three sentences, each of which includes an *adjective* and a *pronoun*.

5–6 _____

_____

7–8 _____

_____

9–10 _____

_____

Write a more powerful *verb* for each of these *verbs*.

Example: look   *stare*

11 drink   _____

12 catch   _____

13 smell   _____

14 speak   _____

30

Sort these *nouns* into the correct columns in the table.

15–20 Wednesday   batch   kite

mosquito   Buckingham Palace   bunch

Common nouns	Proper nouns	Collective nouns

Test 18: **Comprehension**

Read this information carefully.

Great Balls of Gas   *by Robin Kerrod*

1 Stars look like tiny bright specks in the night sky. But they are not tiny at all. They are in fact huge balls of searing hot gas. Stars look small only because they lie many
5 million, million kilometres away. If you could get close to a star, you would find that it looked like our Sun, because the Sun is a star too.

How big are stars?

10 We can measure the size of one star directly because it is so close. This is our own star, the Sun. The Sun measures nearly 1,400,000 kilometres across. Astronomers can work out the size of other stars too.
15 They have discovered that there are many stars smaller than the Sun, and also many much larger. Astronomers call the Sun a dwarf star. They know of red giant stars tens of times bigger.

20 ### Why do stars twinkle?

When we look up at the heavens, we can see thousands of stars shining down, but they do not give out a steady light. They seem to twinkle, or change
25 brightness all the time. In fact they do shine steadily but air currents in the Earth's atmosphere make the starlight bend this way and that. Some of the light gets into our eyes and some is bent away.
30 So, to us on Earth, the stars seem to twinkle.

Do stars last forever?

Just like living things, stars are born, grow older and, in time, die. After shining
35 steadily for some time the stars swell up into a red giant. Some red giants shrink into a white, then a black, dwarf. This will happen to the Sun one day. Other stars swell up from a red giant to a supergiant
40 before exploding as a supernova.

Answer these questions about the extract.

1 What are stars?

_____

2 Why do stars look so small?

_____

3 Which star is the easiest to measure?

_____

4 What type of star do astronomers call the Sun?

_____

5–6 In your own words describe why stars twinkle.

_____

_____

_____

7 When referring to stars, what is a 'red giant'?

_____

_____

8 The information on stars asks and answers three questions. Write two more questions relating to stars that you would like to know the answers to.

(1) _____

_____

(2) _____

_____

Test 19: Mixed

Underline the words that are spoken.

1. "Where is your hat?" called Dad.

2. Angus screamed, "Watch out!"

3. "Let's go to the beach," suggested Maria.

4. "I can't wait until my birthday," said Joe.

Put a tick next to the words spelt correctly and a cross next to those spelt incorrectly.

5. suprise ☐

6. thought ☐

7. difficult ☐

8. exercise ☐

9. imagin ☐

10. accidentaly ☐

Underline the correct form of the *verb* to complete each sentence.

11   I did/done my homework quickly.

12   We was/were late for the party.

13   We did/done an excellent presentation.

14   I was/were tired after swimming.

Underline the *root word* in each of these words.

15   endless

16   printer

17   bicycle

18   trickery

19   collector

20   unclean

TEST 20: Sentences

Copy these sentences, adding the missing commas.

1. Riding on the tractor Kyle felt like a farmer just like his uncle.

2. The puppies chewed shoes furniture and their beds!

3. The ponies jumped the fence cantering up the lane towards the busy road.

4. Meena's sandwiches were filled with cheese ham and mayonnaise.

Write these words as a single word with a *contraction*.

Example: they have — *they've*

5. can not _____

6. could have _____

7. I will _____

8. is not _____

9. have not _____

Copy this passage, adding the missing capital letters.

10–17 chris rushed out of the front door and headed down thresher lane. he was late for football again. ken, the coach, had threatened to throw him off the team if he didn't show for practice. why was it that his mum, liz, always arrived home late on a tuesday?

Write three sentences, each with a *fronted adverbial*.

18 _____

19 _____

20 _____

Time for a break! Go to Puzzle Page 42

Puzzle 1

Add a letter to each empty space to find the answer.
Each word contains the letters OUGH.

The clues will help!

Clue	
A container from which animals eat or drink	___ ___ O U G H
A number	___ O U G H ___
A mixture of flour and water	___ O U G H
Looked for	___ O U G H ___
To dig over	___ ___ O U G H
A short, loud noise from your throat	___ O U G H
A serious shortage of water	___ O U G H ___
An idea or opinion in your mind	___ ___ O U G H ___

Puzzle 2

Pair up a group of letters from each column to make a six-letter word.

nar	_narrow_	nal
sig	_____	ugh
lov	_____	cle
tho	_____	son
cir	_____	rge
sch	_____	row
fri	_____	ief
les	_____	ely
cha	_____	dow
bel	_____	ght
win	_____	ool

Puzzle 3

With a line, match the *definition* with the correct word.

tricycle

duet

decade

double

century

triplets

quartet

duel

a song sung by two people

a three-wheeled bike

three babies born at a similar time to the same mother

a fight between two people

a group of four musicians

a hundred years

two of the same thing

a ten-year period

Puzzle 4

Look carefully at these words. Put them in the correct place in the table.

China, swan, sadly, climb, ours, carelessly, pack, delicious, she, miserable, jump, expensive, calmly, herd, Barney, sleet, apple, Manchester, crowd, they, choose

Nouns		
Common	Proper	Collective

Verbs	Adjectives	Pronouns	Adverbs

Puzzle 5

Try this homophone hunt.

b	j	r	s	t	r	t	w
i	f	d	u	e	e	t	b
a	w	a	i	t	i	h	r
f	l	o	u	r	g	r	o
s	o	n	i	m	n	o	u
g	k	t	b	t	s	n	l
h	e	n	n	b	e	e	n
e	y	s	o	m	s	a	v

Find a *homophone* in the wordsearch for each of the following words.

Write the words you have found.

bean　　　＿＿＿＿＿＿＿＿＿

rain　　　＿＿＿＿＿＿＿＿＿

quay　　　＿＿＿＿＿＿＿＿＿

flower　　＿＿＿＿＿＿＿＿＿

dew　　　＿＿＿＿＿＿＿＿＿

weight　　＿＿＿＿＿＿＿＿＿

thrown　　＿＿＿＿＿＿＿＿＿

Key words

Some special words are used in this book. You will find them picked out in *italics*. These words are explained here.

adjectival phrase	a group of words describing a noun
adjective	a word that describes somebody or something
adverb	a word that gives extra meaning to a verb
adverbial phrase	a word or phrase that makes the meaning of a verb, adjective or another adverb more specific, for example, The Cheshire cat vanished quite slowly, beginning with the end of its tail.
alphabetical order	words arranged in the order of the letters in the alphabet
antonym	a word with a meaning opposite to another word, for example, hot/cold
collective noun	a word referring to a group of things, for example, a *swarm* of bees
compound word	a word made up of two other words, for example, football
conjunction	a word used to link sentences, phrases or words, for example, and, but
contraction	two words shortened into one with an apostrophe placed where the letter/s have been dropped, for example, do not/don't
definition	the meaning of a word
diminutive	a word implying smallness, for example, duckling
fronted adverbial	an adverbial that has been moved before the verb, for example, The day after tomorrow, I'm going on holiday.
homonym	a word that has the same spelling or sound as another word but a different meaning, for example, turn *left*, we *left* the room
homophone	a word that has the same sound as another but a different meaning or spelling, for example, right/write
noun	a naming word for a person, place, feeling or thing
phrase	a group of words that act as a unit
plural	more than one, for example, cats
prefix	a group of letters added to the beginning of a word, for example, un, dis
pronoun	a word that can be used instead of a noun, for example, his
proper noun	the specific name or title of a person or a place, for example, Ben, London
root word	a word to which a prefix or suffix can be added to make another word, for example, quick – *quick*ly
singular	one of something, for example, cat
suffix	a group of letters added to the end of a word, for example, ly, ful
synonym	a word with a very similar meaning to another word, for example, quick/fast
verb	a 'doing' or 'being' word

Progress Grid

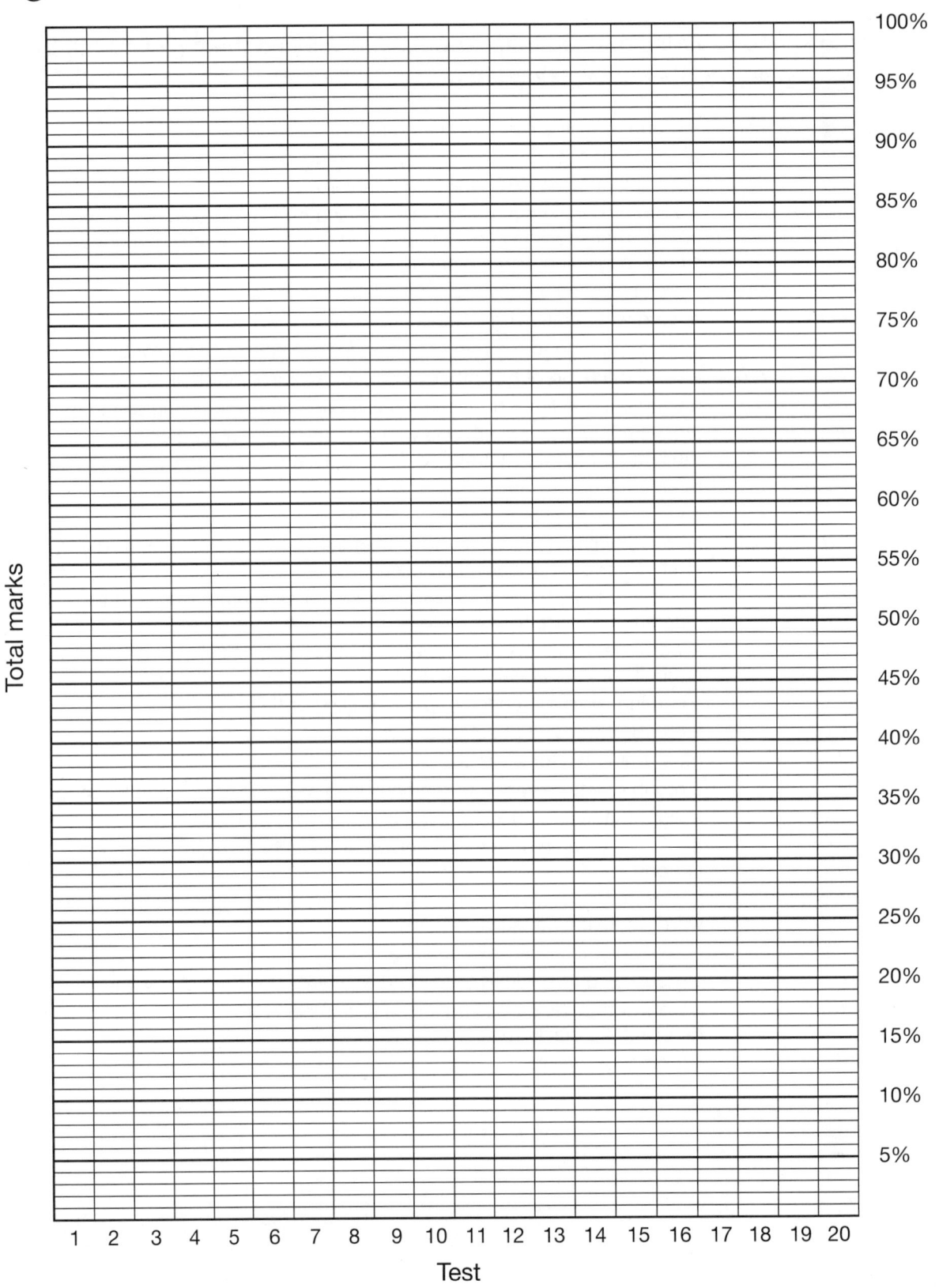

44

Answers

Answers will vary for questions that require children to answer in their own words. Possible answers to most of these questions are given in *italics*.

Test 1: Mixed

1. excit<u>able</u>
2. flex<u>ible</u>
3. agree<u>able</u>
4. forgiv<u>able</u>
5. revers<u>ible</u>
6. avoid<u>able</u>
7. mine
8. theirs
9. ours
10. his
11. *whisper*
12. *move*
13. *break*
14. *frown*
15. *noise*
16. *inside*
17. "Have you fed the dog this morning**?**" asked Mum**.**
18. Dad moaned**,** "Time I mowed the lawn again."
19. "Can we go swimming this afternoon**?**" Alex and Tom pleaded**.**
20. Poppy said**,** "I can't wait until your birthday party."

Test 2: Spelling

1. league
2. unique
3. antique
4. tongue
5. fas©inate
6. cres©ent
7. s©ent
8. dis©ipline
9. s©issors
10. s©ience
11. flannel
12. sparrow
13. yellow
14. kettle
15. saddle
16. wriggle
17. pollute
18. lesson
19. scheme
20. machine
21. character
22. brochure
23. shelf
24. echo
25. chorus

Test 3: Spelling

1. new
2. scene
3. board
4. side
5. sauce
6. deer
7. peace
8. churches
9. valleys
10. knives
11. babies
12. clocks
13. cafés
14. kilos
15. dishes
16. height
17. awful
18. favourite
19. quarter
20. naughty
21. address
22. famous
23. various
24. library
25. rose

Test 4: Comprehension

1. It was her birthday.
2. Anne lived in Amsterdam.
3. Margot was three years older than Anne.
4. Anne's best present was a diary.
5. *Anne was delighted with this present as, for her, the diary was a new friend with whom she could trust everything.*
6. Anne wrote to Kitty for more than two years.
7. *The Netherlands had been under the control of the Germans for two years* OR *Germany had conquered the Netherlands two years earlier.*
8. *Anne might have been excited and touched that so many people were interested in her life and what she'd written.*

Test 5: Vocabulary

1. gangster
2. garage
3. garden
4. garlic
5. gateau
6. *a place where people learn*
7. *a hollow pipe*
8. *a furry animal with long ears*
9. *a fully grown man, woman or animal*
10. *a unit of time, 60 minutes*
11–15. anywhere, cardboard, redhead, waterfall, classroom
16. *busy*
17. *mad*
18. *sprint*
19. *mend*
20. *dislike*

Test 6: Mixed

1. Let's
2. I'll
3. There's
4. we've
5. can't
6. The dogs chased the balls.
7. Schools are closed on Tuesdays.
8. The Sun shone and made the flowers grow.
9. The cars sped down the country lanes.
10–14. prince, gander, duke, nephew, waiter
15. rhyme
16. mystery
17. gym
18. physical
19. myth
20. encyclopedia

Test 7: Grammar

1. flap
2. scream
3. growl
4. scratch
5. *squeaky*
6. *haunted*
7. *bouncy*
8. *muddy*
9. *torn*
10–11. *calmly, quickly*
12–14. Roald Dahl, Jupiter, Tower of London
15. while
16. after
17. but
18. because
19. so
20. and

Test 8: Comprehension

1. Bertie lived in South Africa.
2. Bertie was sitting high in the branches of a tree.
3. The lion cub was very unusual as it was white.
4. Bertie's dad was cross with Bertie as he felt there was no such thing as a white lion cub but Bertie kept arguing that there was.
5. Bertie also saw zebras and wildebeest.
6. Bertie began to doubt himself as day after day he waited for the lion cub and it didn't return.

Bond 10 Minute Tests: English 8–9 years

7 Line 54 'Bertie's heart stopped.'
8 He might go out on his own searching for the white lion cub.

Test 9: Mixed

1–6 Najib called to his friend, "Quick, if we don't hurry we will miss the party!" Henry wasn't sure he wanted to go all the way to Stafford but he grabbed his jumper anyway. "Coming, I'm coming," he moaned.
7 It's **9** It's
8 its **10** its
11–13 bouquet, tribe, flock
14 deliv<u>ery</u>
15 prim<u>ary</u>
16 machin<u>ery</u>
17 mem<u>ory</u>
18 Janu<u>ary</u>
19 laborat<u>ory</u>
20 discov<u>ery</u>

Test 10: Spelling

1 <u>non</u>sense
2 <u>re</u>call
3 <u>un</u>fair
4 <u>un</u>aware   **15** ✓
5 <u>dis</u>honest   **16** ✗
6 <u>dis</u>continue   **17** ✗
7 <u>re</u>visit   **18** ✓
8 <u>dis</u>ability   **19** expansion
9 ✓   **20** simply
10 ✗   **21** magician
11 ✗   **22** angrily
12 ✓   **23** confusion
13 ✗   **24** preparation
14 ✗   **25** television

Test 11: Spelling

1 poisonous   **6** vigorous
2 outrageous   **7** dangerous
3 mountainous   **8** nervous
4 joyous   **9** humorous
5 perilous   **10** courageous

11 fraction   **19** thief
12 invitation   **20** piece
13 direction   **21** field
14 decision   **22** weigh
15 mention   **23** eight
16 occasion   **24** vein
17 television   **25** ceiling
18 subtraction

Test 12: Sentences

1 ?   **4** ?
2 .   **5** !
3 !   **6** .
7 Tania whispered, **"**Quiet or we will wake Grandad.**"**
8 **"**Where is the best place to fish?**"** Tom asked Yousef.
9 Helen giggled, **"**Why are you wearing that strange-looking hat?**"**
10 **"**I love you,**"** said Seamus as he cuddled his puppy.
11 *The terrified spider froze as the bird flew by.*
12 *The cuddly baby giggled as its grandmother gave it a hug.*
13 *Tim stopped to watch as a fast, red car sped down the lane.*
14 *Sarah ran from the monster, trying to hide in the dark, cold shadow of the castle wall.*
15 the two horses' reins
16 the four boys' hats
17 the five pupils' books
18 the Prime Minister's socks
19 the twelve cars' wheels
20 the old man's shoes

Test 13: Comprehension

1 The poem is about a visit to a leisure centre with a swimming pool.
2 The poet notices the bright lights, the chlorine smell, the warmth from the steam and the noise from the children. (Answer needs to highlight three things noticed.)

3 cute
4 The children are thinking whether they can afford a fizzy drink.
5 It is hard to get dressed when you shake and quiver when you are cold and wet.
6 'Eyes are slowly closing' describes how tired the visitors are on their way home.
7 *toe stub, eye poke, crowds, noise.*
8 The poem is titled 'Leisure Centre, Pleasure Centre' because it is about how much pleasure the leisure centre gives to visitors.

Test 14: Mixed

1 thorough – borough
2 rough – tough
3 nought – thought
4 though – dough
5 plough – bough
6 *a book that gives the meaning of words*
7 *a book containing a daily record of personal experiences or observations*
8 *commonplace, usual*
9 *the second month in the year*
10 *the edge of an area*
11 At last Dad arrived home <u>so</u> we could eat our tea.
12 The wind rustled in the trees <u>as</u> darkness fell.
13 Jemma concentrated hard on her game of chess <u>because</u> it was an important match.
14 Daxa picked up the bags <u>and</u> carried them into the house.
15 The phone rang <u>but</u> nobody was home.
16 Lia packed her hairbrush**,** nightie and toothbrush.
17 Despite the tent being hot and stuffy**,** Abi found it fairly comfortable.

Bond 10 Minute Tests: English 8–9 years

18–19 When Daniel returned from school he did his homework**,** piano practice**,** walked the dog and cleaned the fish tank.
20 Sarah ran down the lane**,** her school bag bumping against her leg.

Test 15: Vocabulary

1 *finish*
2 *pull*
3 *sad*
4 *punishment*
5 *stiff*
6 *tarantula*
7 *target*
8 *tarnish*
9 *tart*
10 *tartan*
11 duckling
12 piglet
13 gosling
14 *My grandfather used to work in a coal mine.*
15 *That football is mine, not yours.*
16 dress – frock
17 glasses – spectacles
18 schoolbag – satchel
19 radio – wireless
20 jug – pitcher

Test 16: Mixed

1 engine
2 fox
3 fly
4 scarf
5 drum
6 *loud, black*
7 *cold, heavy*
8 *young, jumping*
9 *sweet, juicy*
10 exposure
11 mature
12 signature
13 displeasure
14 miniature
15 pressure
16 Kate's homework
17 my country's flag
18 Liam's computer
19 Meena's cakes
20 the birds' nests

Test 17: Grammar

1 noisily
2 awkwardly
3 sleepily
4 hastily
5–10 Three different sentences, e.g. *My silly friend Paul likes to wear his clothes inside out.*
11 *gulp*
12 *grab*
13 *sniff*
14 *chat*
15–20

Common nouns	Proper nouns
kite mosquito	Wednesday Buckingham Palace
Collective nouns	
batch bunch	

Test 18: Comprehension

1 Stars are huge balls of searing hot gas.
2 Stars look small because they lie many million kilometres away.
3 The Sun is the easiest star to measure as it is the closest star to Earth.
4 The Sun is a dwarf star.
5–6 *Stars twinkle because the light they shine bends. Some of the light bends and we can see it but some of it bends away from Earth and we can't see it. This makes it looks like the stars are twinkling.*
7 A 'red giant' is a star that has swelled up before it changes into a black dwarf or explodes.
8 Child's own questions, e.g. *How hot are stars? Why do some stars explode?*

Test 19: Mixed

1 <u>"Where is your hat?"</u> called Dad.
2 Angus screamed, <u>"Watch out!"</u>
3 <u>"Let's go to the beach,"</u> suggested Maria.
4 <u>"I can't wait until my birthday,"</u> said Joe.
5 ✗
6 ✓
7 ✓
8 ✓
9 ✗
10 ✗
11 did
12 were
13 did
14 was
15 <u>end</u>less
16 <u>print</u>er
17 <u>bicycle</u>
18 <u>trick</u>ery
19 <u>collect</u>or
20 un<u>clean</u>

Test 20: Sentences

1 Riding on the tractor Kyle felt like a farmer**,** which his uncle had once been.
2 The puppies chewed shoes**,** furniture and their beds!
3 The ponies jumped the fence**,** cantering up the lane towards the busy road.
4 Meena's sandwiches were filled with cheese**,** ham and mayonnaise.
5 can't
6 could've
7 I'll
8 isn't
9 haven't
10–17 **C**hris rushed out of the front door and headed down **T**hresher **L**ane. **H**e was late for football again. **K**en, the coach, had threatened to throw him off the team if he didn't show for practice. **W**hy was it that his mum, **L**iz, always arrived home late on a **T**uesday?
18–20 *I have netball practice every Friday. Why do elephants have long trunks? I can't believe I won the lottery!*

A3

Bond 10 Minute Tests: English 8–9 years

Puzzle 1

TROUGH   PLOUGH
NOUGHT   COUGH
DOUGH   DROUGHT
SOUGHT   THOUGHT

Puzzle 2

narrow, signal, lovely, though, circle, school, fright, lesson, charge, belief, window

Puzzle 3

duet – a song sung by two people
century – a hundred years
tricycle – a three-wheeled bike
duel – a fight between two people
triplets – three babies born on or at a similar time to the same mother
quartet – a group of four musicians
double – two of the same thing
decade – a ten-year period

Puzzle 4

| Nouns ||| Verbs | Adjectives | Pronouns | Adverbs |
Common	Proper	Collective				
swan	China	pack	climb	delicious	they	calmly
sleet	Manchester	herd	jump	expensive	she	carelessly
apple	Barney	crowd	choose	miserable	ours	sadly

Puzzle 5

b	j	r	s	t	r	t	w
i	f	d	u	e	e	t	b
a	w	a	i	t	i	h	r
f	l	o	u	r	g	r	o
s	o	n	i	m	n	o	u
g	k	t	b	r	s	n	l
h	e	n	n	b	e	e	n
e	y	s	o	m	s	a	v

been
reign
key
flour
due
wait
throne

A4